1

POWER WORKBOOK

MW00909886

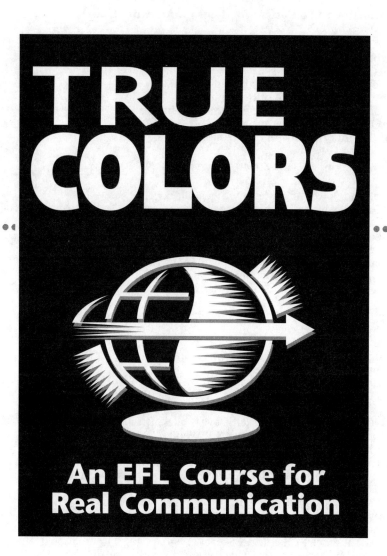

TRUE COLORS

An EFL Course for Real Communication

JAY MAURER

IRENE E. SCHOENBERG

Joan Saslow

Series Director

Longman

longman.com

**True Colors: An EFL Course for Real Communication 1
Power Workbook**

Pearson Education, 10 Bank Street, White Plains, NY 10606

Workbook and Power Activities by Angela Blackwell
Test-Taking Skills by Ken Sheppard and Angela Castro

Editorial directors: Allen Ascher, Pam Fishman
Senior acquisitions editor: Marian Wassner
Development editors: Jessica Miller, Nicole Santos
Director of design and production: Rhea Banker
Executive managing editor: Linda Moser
Marketing manager: Bruno Paul
Senior production editor: Kathleen Silloway
Photo research: Aerin Csigay
Cover design: Rhea Banker, Ann France
Text design: Word & Image Design, Ann France
Text composition: TSI Graphics
Text credits: p. 22, Peter Menzel, *Material World,* San Francisco, 1994:
    Sierra Club Books; p. 55, Samantha Miller, "Brad in profile," *People
    Magazine Online,* December 27, 1996
Text art: Greg Hall, Paul McCusker, Dave McKay, Duśan Petricic,
    Stephen Quinlan, Teco Rodrigues, Jill Wood
Photography: Gilbert Duclos
Photo credits: p. 4, © The Stock Market/(Michael A. Kella Studios Ltd.,
    1994); p. 4, © The Stock Market/(Robert Frenck/Odyssey/Chicago);
    p. 34, © The Stock Market/(Sandy Roessler, 1988); p. 34, © The
    Stock Market/(Jacquelin Austin); p. 34, © The Stock Market /(John
    Henley, 1995); p. 40, copyright Sports 'N Spokes/Paralysed Veterans
    of America, 1994; p. 42, © The Stock Market/(Brent Peterreu);
    p. 47, © The Stock Market/(Ariel Skelley, 1994); p. 49, © International
    Stock/(Elliott Varner Smith); page 55, © (Alpha London)/Globe
    Photos, Inc. (Steve Finn, Apr. 1995); p. PA 10-1, © Scott Gries/Getty
    Images

ISBN: 0-13-184606-X

Printed in the United States of America

4 5 6 7 8 9 10—BAH—08 07 06 05

Contents

To the Teacher

The ***True Colors Power Workbooks*** contain two types of activities that students may do in class or at home.

The **Workbook** sections contain numerous opportunities for written reinforcement of the language taught in the Student's Book. They include a variety of written exercises and activities that give students additional practice in this language. Abundant illustrations serve as prompts. The all-new *Power Activities* that appear as the last two pages of every unit provide a step up in the level of challenge. They focus primarily on grammar and emphasize meaningful and personalized practice. Special *Power Writing* activities give students open-ended or free-response writing practice and usually incorporate grammatical structures taught in the unit.

Two **Test-Taking Skills** sections appear in each ***True Colors Power Workbook:*** one after Unit 5 and one after Unit 10. The questions in these sections are designed to introduce students to the question types and formats they will encounter on the TOEFL and other official examinations while following the language taught at each level of ***True Colors.*** Although the questions in the **Test-Taking Skills** sections do not replicate the TOEFL or any other official test, they can help prepare students for those tests. A chart describing the questions provided in these sections appears on the next page.

Answers to exercises and activities (except personalized and free-response activities) in both the **Workbook** and the **Test-Taking Skills** sections appear on the *True Colors Companion Website* at **www.longman.com/truecolors**.

Test-Taking Skills

Question Category	Question Objective	Question Format
Vocabulary You Should Know (All levels)	Questions test students' knowledge of words taught as active vocabulary in corresponding units of *True Colors*.	Sentence(s) with a space and 4 possible answers. Students must choose the answer that best completes each sentence.
Vocabulary from Context (All levels)	Questions test students' ability to guess from context the meaning of words they do *not* know.	Sentence(s) with an underlined word and 4 possible answers. Students must choose the answer that is closest in meaning to the underlined word.
Sentence Structure (All levels)	Questions test students' ability to recognize correctly structured sentences.	Sentence(s) with a space and 4 possible answers. Students must choose the answer that best completes each sentence.
Error Correction (All levels)	Questions test students' ability to recognize common grammatical errors.	Sentence with 4 underlined words. Students must choose the underlined word that is *not* correct.
Reading: Main Ideas (Levels 1–4)	Questions test students' ability to recognize the main idea of a passage. Questions may ask about the *topic*, *title*, or *main idea*.	Question and 4 answer choices. Students read the passage and circle the answer that states the main idea (and not a detail) of the passage.
Reading: Confirming Content (Levels 1–4)	Questions test students' ability to understand details in a passage. Questions may ask about what is *stated* or *indicated* in the passage or what is true according to the passage.	Question and 4 answer choices. Students circle the letter of the answer that gives the correct information from the passage.
Reading: Making Inferences (Levels 3, 4)	Questions test students' ability to make inferences based on information in the passage. Questions may ask about what conclusions can be drawn about the passage, or what is *likely* or *possible* based on information in the passage.	Question and 4 answer choices. Students circle the letter of the answer that is based on information implied in the passage (but not directly stated in the passage).

Unit 1 Are you in this class?

1 Complete the conversations.

Fill in the blanks with words from the box. You can use some words more than once.

| I'm | He's | She's | We're | They're | It's |

1. **A:** This is Bob. _____He's_____ my neighbor.

   B: Hi, Bob.

2. **A:** Where's Susan?

   B: _____ in the car.

3. **A:** Hi! _____ Alison.

   B: Nice to meet you, Alison.

4. **A:** I'm Kate, and this is Emma. _____ in this class.

   B: Hi. I'm Tom.

5. **A:** How old is Mike?

   B: _____ nine.

6. **A:** Where's the English class?

   B: _____ in room 208.

7. **A:** Who's that?

   B: Adela. _____ Ron's wife.

8. **A:** What do you do?

   B: _____ an engineer.

9. **A:** Where are your friends?

   B: _____ in New York.

❷ Write sentences.

Look at the pictures. Write a sentence for each picture. Use words from the box.

| a doctor | a secretary | an engineer | a nurse | a lawyer | a homemaker |

1. <u>He's an engineer.</u>

2. _____

3. _____

4. _____

5. _____

6. _____

❸ Unscramble the conversation.

Put the conversation in the correct order.

_____ So what do you do, Sally?

___1___ Sally, this is my friend Steve.

_____ I'm an engineer.

_____ Hi, Sally. Nice to meet you.

_____ I'm a teacher. What about you?

_____ Nice to meet you, too.

❹ Write about yourself.

Answer the questions. Tell about yourself. Use short answers.

Example: Are you tall? ___Yes, I am.___

1. Are you short? _____

2. Are you a teenager? _____

3. Are you a student? _____

4. Are you single? _____

5. Are you from the United States? _____

6. Are you married? _____

7. Are you athletic? _____

8. Are you studious? _____

❺ Complete the sentences.

*Fill in the blanks with **a, an,** or **the.***

1. Sandra is _____*a*_____ doctor.

2. _____*The*_____ doctor's name is Felix Yamamoto.

3. Carlos is _____ student at San Fernando College.

4. _____ students in my class are all very nice.

5. He's a nurse? But he's _____ man!

6. _____ new teacher is very young.

7. My friend is _____ artist. He's very good.

8. That's a beautiful picture. _____ artist is Paul Cummings.

9. I live in _____ United States.

6 Match descriptions and pictures.

Look at the pictures. Match each sentence to the correct picture. Write the correct letter in the blank.

a. They're good friends.   **b.** They're married.   **c.** She's studious.

1. _____   **2.** _____   **3.** _____

7 Read and answer questions.

Read the postcard.
Then write the correct answer in the blank.

1. The postcard is to _____Danny_____.
     Jeff / Mexico / Danny

2. The postcard is from _____.
     Danny / Danny's teacher / Danny's mother

3. Danny lives in

   _____.

   Los Angeles / Berkeley / Mexico

4. Danny is

   _____.

   a student / a lawyer / a doctor

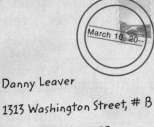

Hi there!
   Mexico is beautiful! Our hotel is really nice. The people are friendly, and the old Mayan ruins are fascinating. And we love the beaches! See you on the 17th. Good luck with your classes!
      Love,
      Mom

March 10, 20--

Danny Leaver
1313 Washington Street, # B
Berkeley, CA 94703

Beach

Ruins

8 Write addresses.

Write the addresses on the envelopes. Pay attention to capital letters.

Note: Illinois = IL   California = CA   Ohio = OH

1. john henry / 2034 rutherford road / champaign il 61821 / usa

2. andrea martin / 140 mission drive / arcadia ca 91006

3. alan mansell / personnel department / worldnet, inc. / 2000 arlington street / columbus oh 43220

POWER ACTIVITIES

1 Vocabulary Power

Which nouns and adjectives go together? Put checks (✓) in the boxes.

	teacher	class	occupation	friend	place
easy	✓	✓	✓		
interesting					
married					
studious					
great					

2 A or An?

*Write **a** or **an**.*

1. __a__ new teacher

2. _____ interesting place

3. _____ young artist

4. _____ old doctor

5. _____ athletic student

6. _____ great job

7. _____ easy class

8. _____ single woman

3 What's the question?

*Make **yes/no** questions.*

1. **A:** I have a new job.

   B: Really? __Is it__ interesting?

2. **A:** Sally's my friend.

   B: _____ in your class?

3. **A:** That's Ryan, and that's Miranda.

   B: _____ married?

4. **A:** This is Keiko.

   B: Nice to meet you. _____ from Japan?

5. **A:** Our teacher is Mr. Green.

   B: _____ young?

6. **A:** I work at Washington High School.

   B: Really? _____ a teacher?

7. **A:** Nadine isn't here.

   B: _____ on vacation?

8. **A:** I'm in a new English class.

   B: _____ hard?

➍ The Verb *Be*

*Read the letter. Fill in the blanks with **am, is, isn't, are,** or **aren't**. Use contractions where possible.*

Greetings from California! We're_____ all very happy in our new
                              1.

home. My job _____ great. It _____ boring at all. The people _____
            2.   **3.**   **4.**

all friendly, and I _____ very happy there.
                   5.

The children _____ both busy at school. Sarah _____ in third
            6.   **7.**

grade and Kevin _____ in first. Kevin _____ quite studious, but Sarah
               8.   **9.**

_____! She _____ athletic.
10.   **11.**

How _____ you? Please come and visit us soon. We _____ very
   12.   **13.**
far away: only 1200 miles!

Love, Amy

➎ Power Writing: People and Things

SUPER Challenge

*Write four true sentences about your friend(s), your teacher(s), yourself, and your class(es).
Use the correct form of the verb **be** and adjectives.*

Example: I'm young and single. _____
••••••

1. My friend(s) _____

2. My teacher(s) _____

3. I'm _____

4. My class(es) _____

Unit 2
There's a noise downstairs!

❶ Circle the correct time.

Look at the clocks. Circle the correct choice.

1. a. It's four o'clock.

   b. It's a quarter to four.

2. a. It's three-fifteen.

   b. It's three forty-five.

3. a. It's two forty-five.

   b. It's a quarter to two.

4. a. It's noon.

   b. It's twelve-thirty.

❷ Unscramble the conversation.

Put the conversation in the correct order.

    1   Hello?

_____   *Fatal Love.* Do you want to go?

_____   Great! Bye!

_____   Hi, Monica. This is Anna.

_____   Really? What is it?

_____   OK. See you there at a quarter after seven.

_____   Oh, hi, Anna! How are you?

_____   Maybe. What time?

_____   I'm fine. Listen. There's a good movie at the Roxie tonight.

_____   It's at seven-thirty.

_____   Bye!

3 Write answers.

Look at the calendar pages.

WEDNESDAY
JULY 7

6 pm meeting
at school

THURSDAY
JULY 8

8 pm movie
Roxie Theater

FRIDAY
JULY 9

7:30 play
Palace Theater

SATURDAY
JULY 10

2:30 rock concert
at the park

SUNDAY
JULY 11

3:00 baseball
game on TV

Answer the questions.

1. Where is the meeting? _It's at school._

2. What time is the meeting? _It's at 6:00._

3. What time is the movie? _____

4. Where is the movie? _____

5. What time is the rock concert? _____

6. Where is the play? _____

7. What time is the baseball game? _____

8. What time is the play? _____

9. Where is the rock concert? _____

4 Complete the sentences.

*Fill in the blanks with **is** or **are**.*

1. There _____is_____ a good movie on TV tonight.

2. There _____are_____ three girls in my family.

3. There _____ twenty computers in the school.

4. There _____ a burglar in the house.

5. There _____ water on the table.

6. There _____ a good play at the theater.

7. There _____ three bedrooms in the house.

8. There _____ milk in the glass.

9. There _____ rice for dinner tonight.

⑤ Match questions and answers.

Match the questions with the answers.

1. ___d___ What movie is at the Lido tonight? **a.** I'm fine.

2. _____ I'm Allen. What's your name? **b.** It's ten to seven.

3. _____ Are you married? **c.** It's at the Palace Theater.

4. _____ Is he married? **d.** *Fatal Love.*

5. _____ What time is it? **e.** I'm Paul, and this is Cindy.

6. _____ Where's the concert? **f.** Yes, I am.

7. _____ How are you? **g.** No, he isn't. He's single.

⑥ Rewrite a message.

Write the message with correct punctuation.

hi julie
how are you theres a great movie at the roxie its called *true love* its at six oclock do you
want to go with me
sara

7 Read and answer questions.

A. Look at the advertisement for a movie. Answer the questions. Use short answers.

Questions	Answers
1. What movie is it?	Loving You.
2. What time is the movie?	
3. Who's in the movie?	
4. Where is the movie?	

B. Now write your own questions about this movie.

Questions	Answers
1. _____?	*Escape from Philadelphia.*
2. _____?	Kurt Costner.
3. _____?	At the Galaxy Theater.
4. _____?	At 1:10, 4:30, and 7:50.

⑧ Write sentences.

A. *Circle the things that you see in the picture.*

supermarkets   (water)   trees   restaurants

a theater   a museum   a zoo   an airport

a university   schools   houses

Challenge

B. *Now write sentences about the picture. Use* **there is** *and* **there are.**

Example: *There is a museum in the picture.*

1. _____

2. _____

3. _____

4. _____

5. _____

POWER ACTIVITIES

❶ Who? What? Where?

Write the correct expression for each picture. Two expressions will not be used.

~~Where's that?~~	What's this?	Who's that?
What's that?	Who's this?	Where's this?

1. <u>Where's that?</u>

2. _____

3. _____

4. _____

❷ Pronouns

Fill in the blanks with **this, there, it,** or **he / she.**

1. _____There_____ 's a new restaurant on King Street. _____It_____ 's very good.

2. Michelle, this is Fernando. _____'s from Chile.

3. Melissa is on the phone. _____'s scared because _____'s a noise downstairs.

4. _____'s two o'clock in the morning!

5. Hi! _____ is Jenny. _____'s a new movie at the Odeon. _____'s at seven o'clock. Can you come?

❸ *There Is, There Are*

*A. Write **T** (true) or **F** (false).*

1. _F_ There are 12 players on a soccer team.

2. ____ There are 50 states in the United States.

3. ____ There are over 8,000,000 people in Mexico City.

4. ____ There is water on the Moon.

5. ____ There are seven days in a week.

6. ____ There are 28 letters in the English alphabet.

7. ____ There is snow in Greenland.

8. ____ There are five planets.

B. Now correct the four false statements.

1. There aren't 12 players on a soccer team. There are 11.

2. _____

3. _____

4. _____

❹ Power Writing: Events This Week

*Write about three events at your school or in your city this week. Use **There is, There's,** or **There are,** and say where and when.*

Example: There's a movie at the Lido tonight.

OR There's a movie at the Lido at 7:30 tonight.

_____

_____

_____

For computer questions, press one now.

❶ Identify the speaker.

*Who is speaking? Write **teacher**, **mother**, or **friend**.*

teacher

mother

friend

"Open your books to page 47."

1. _____teacher_____

"Don't be late for dinner."

2. _____

"Please help me with my homework."

3. _____

"Do page 24 for homework."

4. _____

"Be home at 11:00 P.M.!"

5. _____

"Don't tell my mother!"

6. _____

❷ Match beginnings and endings.

Find the second part of each sentence. Write the correct letter in the blank.

1. ___b___   We're not at home. Please leave   **a.** late.

2. _____   Jeannie, call   **b.** a message.

3. _____   Do you want to go   **c.** a video tonight.

4. _____   Do you have a problem? Talk   **d.** for a walk?

5. _____   Let's watch   **e.** to the teacher.

6. _____   Don't hang   **f.** your mother.

7. _____   Don't be   **g.** up! Stay on the line.

❸ Complete the conversation.

*Fill in the blanks in the conversation. Use **Let's** or **Do you want to**.*

A: ___Do you want to___ go out tonight?
            1.

B: Good idea. How about a movie?

A: OK. _____ go to the Roxie.
           2.

B: What's playing at the Roxie?

A: I don't know. _____ look in the newspaper. . . *Fatal Love*.
                3.

_____ see that?
      4.

B: No, not really. Forget the movie. How about a restaurant? _____ eat out?
                                                5.

A: Sure. Where?

B: How about Enrico's? It's Italian. It's good.

A: OK. _____ walk?
           6.

B: No, I'm tired. _____ drive instead.
                7.

❹ Complete the sentences.

Fill in each blank with a possessive adjective.

1. Ellen is in _____*her*_____ room.

2. I can't go out now! _____ hair is wet!

3. This is for Tom. _____ birthday is tomorrow.

4. Give me that! That's _____ book!

5. Hello. I'm Patty. What's _____ name?

6. My parents are out tonight. It's _____ wedding anniversary.

7. Today is _____ birthday. I'm six.

8. Hi. I'm Manny, and this is _____ wife, Sylvia.

9. The children are at the movies with _____ friends.

10. What a pretty cat! What's _____ name?

❺ Rewrite sentences.

Rewrite the sentences with the correct punctuation.

1. its johns birthday on monday

_____It's John's birthday on Monday._____

2. marys party is on wednesday

_____

3. thats mr johnsons house

_____

4. its my parents anniversary tomorrow

_____

5. the childrens party is next friday

_____

6 Write sentences.

Look at the pictures. Write sentences with possessive nouns.

David   **Samantha**   **Alex**

mug

glasses

1. It's Alex's mug.

2. They're David's glasses.

armchair

CD player

3. _____

4. _____

T-shirt

newspaper

5. _____

6. _____

➐ Complete the puzzle.

Look at the pictures. Write the correct word or words across each line. What's the extra word?

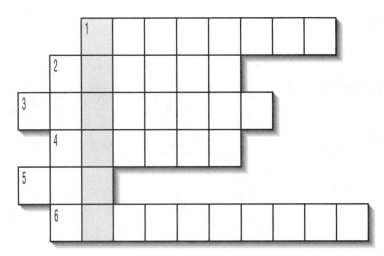

1.
2.
3.
4.
5.
6.

The extra word is _____.

➑ Write the answers.

Look at the family tree. Then answer the questions.

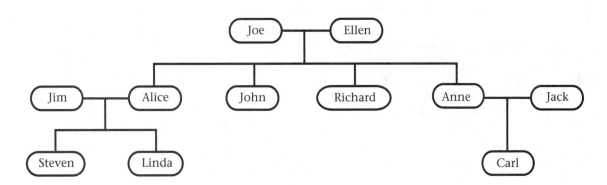

1. Who is Joe's wife? _____ Ellen _____

2. Who are Richard's sisters? __Alice__ and __Anne__

3. Who are Ellen's daughters? _____ and _____

4. Who is Linda's grandfather? _____

5. Who are Alice's brothers? _____ and _____

6. Who is Carl's grandmother? _____

7. Who is Alice's son? _____

POWER ACTIVITIES

❶ Possessive Adjectives

*Rewrite the phrases with **his, her,** or **their.***

1. Jane's brother   *her brother*

2. Tom's wife

3. the children's party

4. Mr. Simpson's son

5. Amelia's address

6. my parents' anniversary

7. Kate's mother

8. Richard's car

❷ Conversation

Fill in the blanks with the correct words from the box. Use each word only once.

about	Don't	Their	instead
Let's	not	want	~~I'm~~

A: Hi, honey, _____*I'm*_____ home.
                1.

B: Hi! Are you hungry?

A: Yes! _____ go to a restaurant.
           2.

B: No, let's _____ go out. Let's eat at home _____.
               3.   **4.**

A: All right. Do you _____ to order a pizza?
                        5.

B: OK. How _____ Mario's?
               6.

A: No. _____ call Mario's. Call Victorio's. _____ pizza is great!
            7.   **8.**

❸ Power Writing: Families

A. Read the description of the Jones family. Fill in the names on the diagram.

There are three children in my family: me (Jackie), my brother Stephen, and my sister Ashley. Our parents' names are Gloria and Philip. My husband's name is Rob, and our children are Emma and Steve. My brother Stephen is married too. His wife's name is Vanessa. They don't have children. My sister Ashley isn't married.

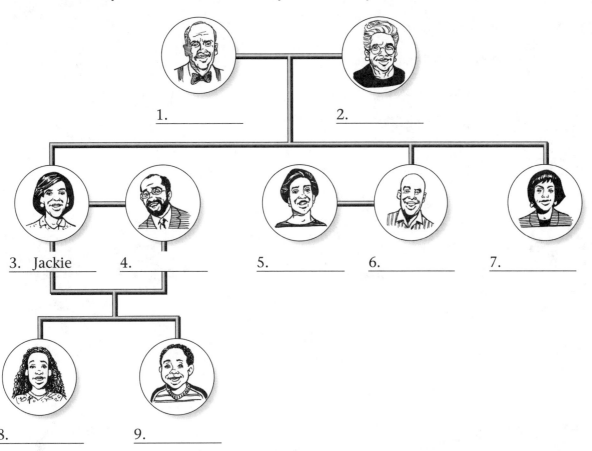

1. _____   2. _____

3. Jackie _____   4. _____   5. _____   6. _____   7. _____

8. _____   9. _____

*B. Now write a description of your family. Use possessive adjectives and possessive nouns. You can begin like this or in your **own** way.*

There are _____ children in my family: _____

_____

_____

_____

_____

Unit 4

What's Bob doing?

❶ Match statements and pictures.

Look at the pictures. Match each sentence with the correct picture.

1. ___e___   They're playing ball.

2. _____   He's studying.

3. _____   She's talking to a friend.

4. _____   He's exercising.

5. _____   He's fixing the car.

6. _____   She's watching TV.

a.

b.

c.

d.

e.

f.

2 Complete the sentences.

Complete each sentence with the correct word from the box. Use some words more than once.

playing	doing	going	making	watching

1. I'm _____doing_____ my homework.

2. We're _____ tennis.

3. I'm _____ dinner.

4. He's _____ for a walk.

5. They're _____ a video.

6. They're _____ baseball.

7. Amy is _____ TV.

8. Mom is _____ pizza.

3 Complete the paragraph.

Look at the picture. Write the correct form of the verb in the blank.

It's Saturday afternoon in Bellville. The sun _____*is shining*_____. The Munson

                                           1. shine

family is at home. Gloria Munson _____ a book. Her son Peter

                                   2. read

and his friend _____ basketball. Alice, her daughter, _____ on

                    3. play   **4.** talk

the phone. Baby Anne _____. Gloria's husband, Tom, _____ a

                    5. sleep   **6.** fix

bicycle. Adam, from Sal's Pizza, _____ a pizza. Two people _____

                    7. deliver   **8.** walk

down the street. The Munson's neighbors _____ their car.

                                          9. wash

④ Write questions.

*Alice is talking to her grandmother in Florida.
Read their conversation. Write the questions.*

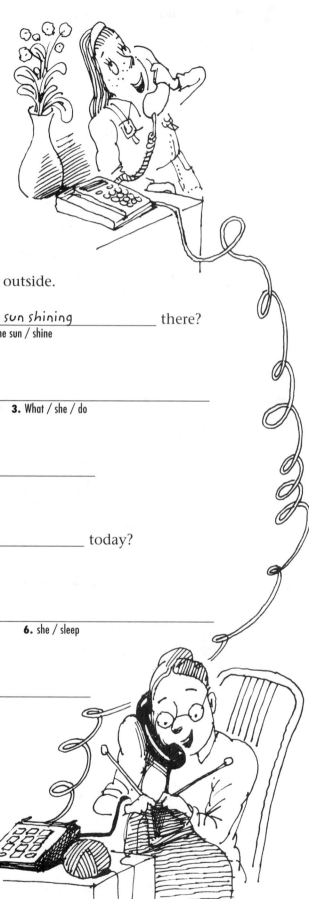

A: Grandma? This is Alice.

B: Alice! What a nice surprise! Hello, dear.

_____ *What are you doing?* _____
1. What / you / do

A: Oh, nothing.

B: Where are you?

A: I'm at home. I'm inside. But everyone else is outside.

B: Outside? It's raining here. _____ *Is the sun shining* _____ there?
2. the sun / shine

A: Yes, it's a beautiful day.

B: And what about your Mom? _____
3. What / she / do

A: She's reading.

B: That's nice. _____
4. What / she / read

A: A new book.

B: And your Dad? _____ today?
5. What / he / do

A: He's here. He's fixing his bike.

B: That's good. How's the baby? _____
6. she / sleep

A: Yes, she's sleeping now. She's fine.

B: And Peter? _____
7. What / he / do

A: He's with his friend Mario.

B: _____
8. What / they / do

A: Playing basketball. What about you, Gran?

_____
9. What / you / do

B: I'm making a sweater for your baby sister.

⑤ Write ordinal numbers.

Unscramble the words.

DRITH   _____*third*_____   TOURFH   _____

THENT   _____   NOSCED   _____

THIFF   _____   THISX   _____

THINN   _____   STIRF   _____

VENSETH   _____   THIGHE   _____

⑥ Complete the sentences.

Write the correct object pronouns in the blanks.

1. Where's Anne? There's a phone call for _____*her*_____.

2. John, listen to me! I'm talking to _____!

3. That's my book! Give it to _____!

4. My homework? I'm doing _____ now.

5. Alice and John? We're meeting _____ tonight.

6. My sister's in Kenya. I'm writing a letter to _____ now.

7. We're watching a movie. Come and watch it with _____!

8. That's a good book. We're reading _____ in class.

9. The children are going to the baseball game. Let's go with _____.

10. Anita is at Luigi's Pizza, and Josh is with _____.

11. You're going to New York? Is your wife going with _____?

12. We're lost. Please give _____ directions.

7 Write answers.

A. Look at the map.
Then answer the questions that follow.

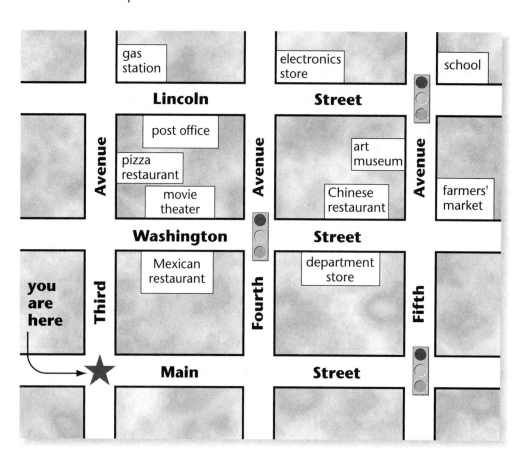

1. Where is the electronics store?

   It's on Lincoln Street, at the corner of Fourth Avenue.

2. Where is the gas station?

_____

3. Where is the Mexican restaurant?

_____

4. Where is the Chinese restaurant?

_____

5. Where is the farmers' market?

_____

B. *Now read the directions. Start at* **Main Street and Third Avenue.**

1. Walk down Main Street to Fifth Avenue. Turn left. It's between Washington Street and Lincoln Street, on the left.

What is it? _____ It's the art museum. _____

2. Go down Third Avenue to Lincoln Street. Turn right. It's between Third Avenue and Fourth Avenue, on the right.

What is it? _____

3. Go to the corner of Main Street and Fourth Avenue. Turn left on Fourth Avenue. Go one block. Turn right on Washington Street. It's between Fourth Avenue and Fifth Avenue, on the right.

What is it? _____

4. Walk down Main Street to Fifth Avenue. Turn left on Fifth Avenue. Walk two blocks. It's on the right, on the corner of Lincoln Street and Fifth Avenue.

What is it? _____

5. Go down Third Avenue to Washington Street. It's on Third Avenue, between Washington Street and Lincoln Street, on the right.

What is it? _____

POWER ACTIVITIES

1 Present Continuous: Descriptions

Find six differences between Picture A and Picture B. Write sentences saying what is different.

A

B

1. In A, the man on the bench is reading. In B, he is watching the game.

2. _____

3. _____

4. _____

5. _____

6. _____

2 Present Continuous: Questions and Answers

A. *Answer the questions about yourself **right now**.*

1. What are you doing right now?   I'm watching T.V.

2. Are you at home?   _____

3. Are you alone or with a friend?   _____

4. Are you listening to music?   _____

5. Are there other people in the room?   _____

6. If so, what are they doing?   _____

B. Now write four sentences about what you **aren't** doing right now. Use your imagination!

1. _____

2. _____

3. _____

4. _____

❸ Power Writing: Directions and Descriptions

Make a map of your neighborhood like the one on Workbook page 20. Show the locations of your home and two of the following places. Then write the directions from your house to the places on your map.

a supermarket	a bank	a restaurant
a hospital	a park	a museum

1. To get from my house to _____, go _____

   _____

   _____

   _____

   _____

2. To get to the _____, go _____

   _____

   _____

   _____

   _____

You lose it. We find it.

❶ Choose the correct verb.

Complete the paragraph. Circle the correct form of the verbs.

Masako and Hiro Hayashi (**1.** (live) / lives) in Tokyo, Japan. Hiro (**2.** work / works) in an electronics company. Masako (**3.** work / works) part-time. They have two daughters, Keiko and Tomiko. The girls (**4.** go / goes) to school five days a week. Keiko also (**5.** go / goes) to school on Saturday mornings.

The Hayashis (**6.** eat / eats) breakfast at 6:30. Hiro (**7.** take / takes) the train to work at 7:30. The girls (**8.** leave / leaves) for school at 8:00. Then Masako (**9.** do / does) the shopping. Sometimes she (**10.** visit / visits) a neighbor. Then she (**11.** make / makes) dinner for the family. In the evenings, the girls (**12.** do / does) homework and (**13.** watch / watches) TV. Hiro often (**14.** come / comes) home late.

❷ Match questions and answers.

A. *Match the questions with the answers.*

1.	__d__	What's your name?	**a.** No, part-time. I work full-time.
2.	_____	Do you study full-time?	**b.** Not really. It's a hard job.
3.	_____	What do you do?	**c.** In Belmont. It's near San Francisco.
4.	_____	Do you like your job?	**d.** Alex.
5.	_____	When do you work?	**e.** I'm a taxi driver.
6.	_____	Where do you live?	**f.** Yes, I have a son.
7.	_____	Do you have children?	**g.** Five days a week, twelve hours a day.

B. *Now put the words in the correct order to make six questions about Alex. Then answer the questions, using the information on page 22. Use short answers.*

Questions	Answers
1. Alex / do / does / What	
<u>What does Alex do ?</u>	<u>He's a taxi driver.</u>
2. Alex / Does / full-time / work	
_____	_____
3. he / does / Where / live	
_____	_____
4. work / When / he / does	
_____	_____
5. have / he / a / Does / daughter	
_____	_____
6. his / he / job / Does / like	
_____	_____

❸ Check the boxes.

A. *What do you think about these subjects? Put checks (✔) in the boxes.*

	Easy	Hard	Interesting	Exciting	Boring
art					
business					
computers					
dance					
journalism					
math					
medicine					
music					

(continued on next page)

B. *Now write five sentences.*

      I think art is exciting.

1. _____

2. _____

3. _____

4. _____

5. _____

❹ Write questions.

Read the sentences. Then write questions to complete the conversation.

1. A: ___Where do you work, Anna_____?

    B: I work in the library at City University.

2. A: _____ your job?

    B: Oh, yes. I love it.

3. A: _____ full-time?

    B: No, part-time.

4. A: _____?

    B: I work from ten to two.

5. A: _____?

    B: I live on 35th Street. It's only five blocks from the university.

❺ Write verbs.

Write the third person singular form of each verb in the simple present tense.

1. look ___looks___ **2.** drink _____ **3.** teach _____ **4.** study _____

5. love _____ **6.** get _____ **7.** have _____ **8.** do _____

9. live _____ **10.** watch _____ **11.** worry _____ **12.** speak _____

⑥ Write about Carmen and Anna.

A. Look at the pictures. Fill in the charts.

Carmen's house   **Anna's house**

	Carmen	Anna		Carmen	Anna
1. has a child	✔		**5.** loves to cook		
2. studies part-time			**6.** plays tennis		
3. has a dog			**7.** plays guitar		
4. loves to travel			**8.** wears glasses		

B. Now write about Carmen and Anna.

Carmen

Carmen has a child.

_____

_____

_____

Anna

Anna studies part-time.

_____

_____

_____

Write about yourself.

A. Answer the questions. Tell about yourself.

Example: Do you study full-time?   <u>No, I study part-time.</u>

1. Where do you live? _____

2. Do you live in an apartment? _____

3. Do you live alone? _____

4. What do you do every morning? _____

5. What do you eat for breakfast? _____

6. When do you eat lunch? _____

7. What do you do in the evenings? _____

8. Do you exercise? _____

9. Do you watch TV? _____

10. Do you like music? _____

B. A pen pal is a person who lives far away. Pen pals write letters to each other. Write a postcard to a new pen pal. Write about yourself. Use some of the information from above. Sign the letter with your name.

Dear pen pal,

   My name is _____ and I live in _____

_____

I _____

_____

_____

_____

_____

                                    Sincerely,

                                    _____
                                    (*Sign your name here.*)

POWER ACTIVITIES

1 Simple Present or Present Continuous?

Circle the correct form of the verb.

1. A: What (do you do/are you doing)?

B: I'm a student.

2. A: Hi Matt! What (do you do/are you doing)?

B: Hi Sue! (I fix/I'm fixing) my bicycle.

3. A: My sister is a teacher.

B: Really? (Does she like/Is she liking) it?

4. A: Can I park here?

B: No. Adam always (parks/is parking) here. Park over there instead.

5. A: Is Alison at home?

B: Yes. She (makes/is making) dinner right now.

6. A: How often (do you exercise/are you exercising)?

B: I (go/am going) to the gym about three times a week. What about you?

2 Simple Present: *Wh-* Questions

Write questions for the underlined words.

1. We live <u>near Houston, Texas</u>.   *Where do you live?*

2. <u>My mother</u> works at the university. _____

3. She teaches <u>Spanish</u>. _____

4. My brothers play <u>basketball and soccer</u>. _____

5. They play <u>in the evenings</u>. _____

6. <u>My sister</u> has a part-time job. _____

7. She works <u>at a restaurant</u>. _____

8. I study <u>music</u> three times a week. _____

❸ A Day in the Life of Mark

Read the paragraph. Then fill in the blanks with the simple present, affirmative, or negative form of one of the verbs below. You may use some verbs more than once. Try to use all of the verbs.

drink	get	live	take	eat
drive	go	watch	like	work

Mark is a lawyer. He _____lives_____ in an apartment in West Los Angeles and
             1.

_____ in an office downtown. Every morning he gets up at about seven-thirty,
   2.

_____ a shower, and _____ to work. He _____ breakfast at
   3.   **4.**   **5.**

home. Instead, he _____ a cup of coffee at a coffee shop and _____ it
                6.   **7.**

in his car.

In the evening, Mark often _____ out with his girlfriend, Sonya. Sometimes
                             8.

they _____ to a movie, but they _____ to movies together very much,
      9.   **10.**

because they _____ the same kinds of movies. He _____ TV very
                11.   **12.**

much but he always _____ the news at eleven o'clock.
                 13.

❹ Power Writing: About a Friend

Write a paragraph about a day in the life of someone you know. Use the paragraph in Exercise 3 as a guide.

_____

_____

_____

_____

_____

1 Complete the questions.

*Fill in the blanks with **Do, Does, Are,** or **Is.***

1. _____Do_____ you like your job?

2. _____Is_____ there a concert tonight?

3. _____ it raining?

4. _____ you have a computer?

5. _____ Alex have children?

6. _____ there a post office on Washington Street?

7. _____ you married?

8. _____ they working today?

9. _____ Mario like school?

10. _____ you have grandchildren?

11. _____ there a farmers' market here?

12. _____ Peter work full-time?

2 Match verbs and objects.

Draw lines from each verb to one or two words in the circle.

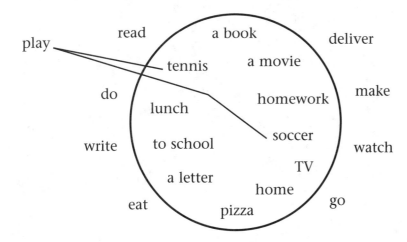

❸ Complete the conversation.

Fill in the blanks with the correct words from the box. Use each word only once.

at	~~from~~	of	on	to

A: John? Is that you? Listen. We're lost.

B: Well, where are you calling ____*from*____?
  1.

A: We're _____ the corner _____ Fifth and Main Street.
  2.   **3.**

B: OK. Go _____ the light. Turn left. We're the third house _____ the right.
  4.   **5.**

A: OK. Thanks. See you soon!

❹ Test your memory.

Take five minutes. Write more words in each category. How many do you remember?

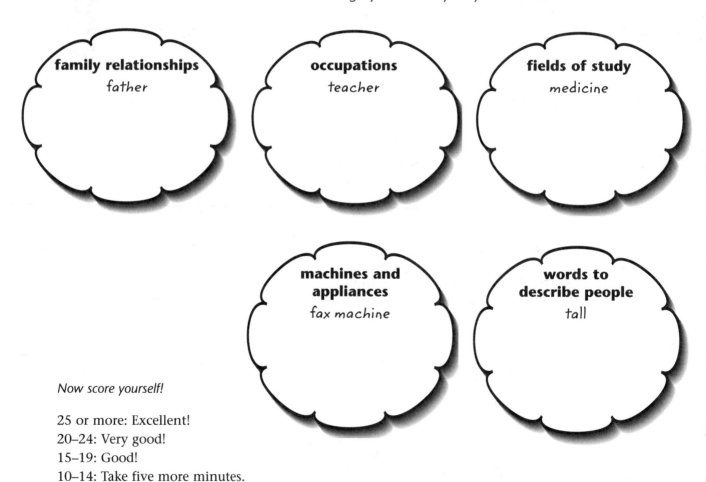

family relationships
father

occupations
teacher

fields of study
medicine

machines and appliances
fax machine

words to describe people
tall

Now score yourself!

25 or more: Excellent!
20–24: Very good!
15–19: Good!
10–14: Take five more minutes.
1–9: Look at Units 1–5 again.

⑤ Write the expression.

Write the correct expression for each picture.

Let's go to a movie.   ~~Sorry I'm late.~~
Nice to meet you.   We're lost.

1. Sorry I'm late.

2. _____

3. _____

4. _____

⑥ Rewrite sentences.

Rewrite the sentences with the correct punctuation.

1. theres a movie at the roxie on wednesday

_____There's a movie at the Roxie on Wednesday._____

2. he doesnt work on saturdays

_____

3. mrs clark is peters grandmother

_____

4. anna is at marias house

_____

TEST-TAKING SKILLS

SECTION I
Vocabulary You Should Know

> 1. Read the sentence(s).
> 2. Try each answer in the space.
> 3. Circle the letter of the answer that best completes the sentence.

1. They're _____ teenagers. They play soccer and basketball.
   - (A) historical
   - (B) athletic
   - (C) single
   - (D) fictional

2. This is my classmate Ana from Brazil. She's _____ history too.
   - (A) playing
   - (B) going
   - (C) watching
   - (D) studying

3. When is the concert? Is it on _____?
   - (A) Sunday
   - (B) snow
   - (C) single
   - (D) sister

4. There's food in the refrigerator. We have meat, milk, and _____.
   - (A) oranges
   - (B) concerts
   - (C) characters
   - (D) directions

5. My new apartment is _____. I really love it.
   - (A) athletic
   - (B) excited
   - (C) hungry
   - (D) terrific

6. Stand up. _____ a partner.
   - (A) Sit
   - (B) Go
   - (C) Open
   - (D) Choose

7. Your VCR isn't broken. Press the button on the _____.
   - (A) secretary
   - (B) engineer
   - (C) watch
   - (D) remote

8. My fax machine and computer aren't _____.
   - (A) working
   - (B) wanting
   - (C) walking
   - (D) watching

9. Where does your sister live? What is _____ phone number?
   - (A) his
   - (B) their
   - (C) her
   - (D) its

10. Is George working at Luigi's new restaurant? Is he _____ pizza?
    - (A) going
    - (B) leaving
    - (C) making
    - (D) closing

11. Paul needs a _____. He's lost.

   (A) neighbor
   (B) CD player
   (C) laptop
   (D) map

12. John and Kay are husband and _____.
    They're married.

   (A) wife
   (B) work
   (C) son
   (D) mother

13. A lot of women are doctors. They work
    in _____.

   (A) journalism
   (B) business
   (C) dance
   (D) medicine

14. Greta _____ German magazines, and
    she watches German operas.

   (A) reads
   (B) gives
   (C) teaches
   (D) works

15. This is _____ story. I like it a lot.

   (A) a hard
   (B) an interesting
   (C) an impossible
   (D) a missing

SECTION 2
Vocabulary from Context

1. Read the sentence(s).
2. Try each answer in place of the underlined word(s).
3. Circle the letter of the best answer.

1. Margaret is a housewife. She stays home
   and works in the house every day.

   (A) an engineer
   (B) a manager
   (C) a nurse
   (D) a homemaker

2. Alice's mother is fascinating. She's a busy
   lawyer, and she loves rock concerts.

   (A) fictional
   (B) interesting
   (C) short
   (D) historical

3. Her last name has fifteen letters. It's
   tough to spell.

   (A) terrific
   (B) right
   (C) busy
   (D) hard

4. There is a noise downstairs and Amanda
   is alone. She is frightened.

   (A) terrific
   (B) scared
   (C) strange
   (D) boring

5. The <u>thief</u> is running away from her house and he has her new laptop!

   (A) student
   (B) burglar
   (C) teacher
   (D) actor

6. This is <u>an entertaining</u> party. We're having a good time.

   (A) a fun
   (B) a historical
   (C) an athletic
   (D) a studious

7. My brother is <u>repairing</u> my fax. He's good with broken machines.

   (A) fixing
   (B) finding
   (C) writing
   (D) doing

8. <u>Push</u> the button on the VCR. It's on the left.

   (A) Stand
   (B) Press
   (C) Watch
   (D) Order

9. TV has too many <u>commercials</u>. There are fifteen to twenty every hour.

   (A) actors
   (B) addresses
   (C) animals
   (D) advertisements

10. I'm <u>starved</u>. I want something to eat, but there's no food in the house.

    (A) studious
    (B) interesting
    (C) hungry
    (D) lost

11. Let's take a <u>stroll</u> after dinner. It's good exercise.

    (A) pizza
    (B) message
    (C) walk
    (D) map

12. <u>Select</u> a partner. Practice the dialogue together.

    (A) Choose
    (B) Make
    (C) Close
    (D) Leave

13. George is very athletic. He's always <u>working out</u> at the gym.

    (A) driving
    (B) exercising
    (C) living
    (D) delivering

14. Six great criminal <u>attorneys</u> work for that law office.

    (A) doctors
    (B) lawyers
    (C) adults
    (D) managers

15. We need milk, bread, and oranges from the <u>grocery store</u>.

    (A) restaurant
    (B) supermarket
    (C) lunch
    (D) homemaker

SECTION 3
Sentence Structure

> 1. Read the sentence(s).
> 2. Try each answer in the space.
> 3. Circle the letter of the answer that best completes the sentence.

1. Hi. _____ Mark Blake. I'm your teacher.

   (A) My name is
   (B) My name
   (C) Name is
   (D) Is my name

2. Philip _____ of a character on TV. Do you know her name?

   (A) is
   (B) is he thinking
   (C) is thinking
   (D) thinking

3. Is he an _____ or a doctor?

   (A) superhero
   (B) artist
   (C) student
   (D) nurse

4. It's a boring movie _____ a woman and her dog.

   (A) at
   (B) in
   (C) about
   (D) on

5. _____ two maps and a CD player in the classroom.

   (A) There are
   (B) There's
   (C) Is there
   (D) They're

6. The concert is starting in five minutes, and _____.

   (A) is he late
   (B) tonight at
   (C) he's late
   (D) is on

7. _____ those people in the photograph in the magazine?

   (A) Who are
   (B) There are
   (C) Why
   (D) Are interesting

8. She is watching _____ on TV tonight.

   (A) playing basketball
   (B) a game
   (C) is basketball
   (D) basketball game

9. _____ studies journalism at the university.

   (A) She is
   (B) Joe's sister
   (C) Does she
   (D) My sisters

10. _____ not watching TV right now.

   (A) I do
   (B) I'm
   (C) I don't
   (D) I

11. My mother _____ math this year.

 (A) not teaching
 (B) is teaching
 (C) teach
 (D) aren't teaching

12. This machine _____ toast in two minutes.

 (A) is it making
 (B) let's make
 (C) make it
 (D) makes

13. What _____ making?

 (A) at home
 (B) he is
 (C) are you
 (D) food

14. My brother hates opera, but _____ rock music.

 (A) really
 (B) doesn't he
 (C) he likes
 (D) about it

15. This soccer game is _____. Our team is winning.

 (A) doesn't worry
 (B) aren't fun
 (C) going to
 (D) really exciting

SECTION 4
Error Correction

> 1. Read the sentence.
> 2. Read the underlined words and the words around them.
> 3. Circle the letter below the word that is not correct.

1. There be twenty or thirty students at the party.
    A   B   C   D

2. Sorry, I busy right now, but call me tomorrow.
       A   B   C   D

3. Does Alice live in a apartment or a house?
    A   B   C   D

4. There are three Brazilian student in my class.
   A   B   C   D

5. Does George watches a lot of movies?
    A   B   C   D

6. Why are them late for class today?
    A   B   C   D

7. Harry's brother is live in Tokyo.
   A   B   C   D

8. Peter is calling <u>him</u> <u>doctor</u> for <u>an</u> appointment.
    A   B   C   D

9. He is <u>speak</u> to a <u>young</u> Italian <u>woman</u>.
  A   B   C   D

10. There <u>are</u> a <u>gas</u> station <u>on</u> <u>the</u> corner.
       A   B   C D

11. <u>Is</u> Joe <u>deliver</u> a <u>pizza</u> right <u>now</u>?
  A   B   C   D

12. <u>Theirs</u> <u>computer</u> is broken, and they <u>are</u> <u>calling</u> the help number.
    A   B   C   D

13. She <u>exercise</u> in the <u>morning</u> and <u>watches</u> TV in <u>the</u> evening.
     A   B   C   D

14. <u>Let's</u> <u>studying</u> <u>our</u> notes from <u>class</u>.
   A   B   C   D

15. That tall <u>woman</u> in <u>our</u> class <u>are</u> always <u>late</u>.
         A   B   C   D

SECTION 5
Reading

> 1. Read the passage.
> 2. Read the question.
> 3. Circle the letter of the best answer.

Questions 1–5

Spring is a wonderful season in Washington, D.C. April and May are warm, sunny months. The grass is green, and the parks are full of flowers. The city is famous for the beautiful cherry blossoms on the trees.

On a nice day in spring, you can see people walking their dogs, talking, or running in the parks. People also enjoy playing tennis and eating at the city's many restaurants.

Tourists come from all over the world. Tour groups visit the Capitol and other important places. Visitors spend many hours at the Smithsonian museums and tour the White House, the president's home. They also visit the Washington Monument, the Lincoln Memorial, and the National Zoo.

Washington, D.C., is a great place to visit on a spring vacation. It is a historical and exciting city.

1. What is the *topic* of this passage?

(A) a place

(B) a tree

(C) a person

(D) an event

2. What is *stated* in the passage about Washington, D.C.?

   (A) Every season is the same.
   (B) Some people don't like it.
   (C) The city has a great baseball team.
   (D) Spring is a good time to visit.

3. According to the passage, what is *true* about Washington, D.C.?

   (A) There is nothing to do there.
   (B) The president lives in the Smithsonian.
   (C) Visitors come from many countries.
   (D) Everyone in Washington, D.C., has a dog.

4. What is *probably true* about the cherry trees?

   (A) Cherry trees have flowers in the winter.
   (B) The president doesn't like cherry trees.
   (C) Visitors come to see the cherry trees.
   (D) Cherry trees only grow in big cities.

5. What is a good *title* for this passage?

   (A) Opinions about Great Cities
   (B) Springtime in Washington, D.C.
   (C) Information about the World
   (D) Vacations for Single People

Questions 6–10

Twenty years ago almost all nurses were women, and almost all pilots were men. Today women fly planes, and men care for patients. The jobs are the same, but now both men and women are working as nurses and pilots.

There are many other examples of changing jobs roles for men and women. Forty years ago there were no women news reporters on television. Now women report the news, the weather, and even men's sports. Women are reporting games and interviewing athletes. Fifty years ago there were almost no women lawyers or doctors, but today over half of all medical students are women.

Today men teach very young children. Men work as librarians and secretaries. Some men stay home to take care of the house and children. They are called "househusbands" or "stay-at-home dads." However, many women still work as homemakers.

Jobs are changing. Today men and women are working in every field.

6. What is the *topic* of this passage?

   (A) jobs for men and women
   (B) schools for nurses and pilots
   (C) finding a job in the United States
   (D) learning to fly an airplane

7. According to the passage, what is *true* today about women?

    (A) Women like to be secretaries.
    (B) All doctors are now women.
    (C) Women report news and sports.
    (D) There are no homemakers today.

8. What is *stated* in the passage about men?

    (A) Only men are sports reporters.
    (B) All lawyers are men.
    (C) Men never take care of the home.
    (D) Some men stay at home with the children.

9. What is *probably true* about men and women today?

    (A) Men like their jobs, but women don't.
    (B) Women don't like sports, but men do.
    (C) There are no women pilots.
    (D) Both men and women take care of children.

10. What is a good *title* for this passage?

    (A) Jobs of Today
    (B) Today's Nurses and Pilots
    (C) Exciting New Jobs for Women
    (D) Where Men and Women Study

Unit 6

We're going to win.

1 Write vocabulary words.

Label the parts of the body.
Use the words in the box.

back	ankle	elbow
arm	hand	shoulder
knee	wrist	

1. _____
2. _____
3. _____
4. _____
5. _____
6. _____
7. _____
8. _____

 Question: What other parts of the body can you name?

_____

2 Complete the sentences.

Complete each sentence. Use **be going to** and the indicated verb. Use contractions with the pronouns.

1. He ___'s going to buy___ a book.
(buy)

2. She _____ a letter.
(write)

3. She _____ a phone call
(make)

4. They _____ a movie.
(watch)

5. They _____ soccer.
(play)

6. It _____.
(rain)

③ Write questions and answers.

Look at Barbara's calendar for tomorrow.

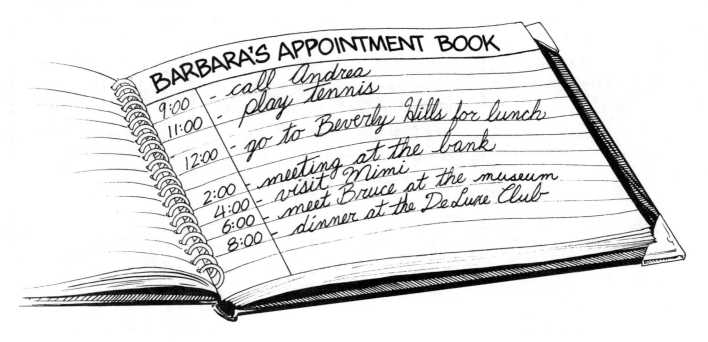

BARBARA'S APPOINTMENT BOOK

9:00 - call Andrea
11:00 - play tennis
12:00 - go to Beverly Hills for lunch
2:00 - meeting at the bank
4:00 - visit Mimi
6:00 - meet Bruce at the museum
8:00 - dinner at the DeLuxe Club

Make questions from these words. Then answer the questions.

Questions   **Answers**

1. What / do / nine o'clock?

   What's she going to do at nine o'clock?   She's going to call Andrea.

2. What / do / eleven o'clock?

_____   _____

3. Where / go/ twelve o'clock?

_____   _____

4. Where / be / two o'clock?

_____   _____

5. What / do / four o'clock?

_____   _____

6. Who / meet / six o'clock?

_____   _____

7. Where / go / eight o'clock?

_____   _____

④ Write about yourself.

What are you going to do? Write five sentences. Use these words:

I'm going to I'm not going to	watch TV do homework go shopping take a vacation go to a movie visit a friend buy food work at home call a friend go to a party eat dinner at home	tonight this evening tomorrow next week on the weekend

Example: _I'm not going to do homework tonight._

I'm going to watch TV this evening.

1. _____

2. _____

3. _____

4. _____

5. _____

⑤ Unscramble the conversation.

Put the conversation in the correct order.

___1___   Doctor's office. Can I help you?

_____   Bye.

_____   Hello, my name is Sarah Lee. I need to see Doctor Martin.

_____   How about four o'clock tomorrow afternoon?

_____   You're welcome. See you then. Good-bye.

_____   Yes. How about eleven o'clock?

_____   Tomorrow afternoon? I'm going to be in class until five. Is the morning a possibility?

_____   Eleven o'clock is fine. Thank you.

6 Complete the sentences.

*Fill in the blanks with **in** or **at**.*

1. Call me. I'm _____at_____ home now.

2. My mother is _____ work.

3. Angela lives _____ the city.

4. Sarah's not _____ school today. I think she's sick.

5. My husband is _____ home today. He's looking after the children.

6. I'm _____ class until 12:00, but I'm free after that.

7 Rewrite sentences.

Rewrite each sentence, using the adverb in parentheses. Be careful with word order!

1. I have coffee in the morning. (always)

I always have coffee in the morning.

2. My husband exercises in the morning. (often)

_____

3. He stays home until 2:00 P.M. (usually)

_____

4. He goes shopping. (sometimes)

_____

5. I am at home before six o'clock. (usually)

_____

6. We watch a movie on TV. (occasionally)

_____

7. We are in bed before eleven. (never)

_____

⑧ Write about yourself.

Use the words from the box. Try to use at least three different words.

always	often	usually	rarely	sometimes	never	occasionally

Example: (have headaches)   I sometimes have headaches.

1. (go to bed before eleven o'clock)   _____

2. (take a bus to work or school)   _____

3. (sleep late on Saturdays)   _____

4. (have toothaches)   _____

⑨ Read and answer questions.

A. *Read the article from the **Cascadia Times** and fill in the chart on the next page.*

New Year, New Starts

What are you going to do differently next year? Here are some people's answers:

Liana Hoffman (27)
Ithaca, New York
I'm going to get more exercise. I'm going to walk to work every day. It's only eight blocks from my home, but I always take the bus. Not next year! I'm also going to take an exercise class after work, with my friend Sue.

Amy Williams (15)
Terre Haute, Indiana
I'm going to help my mom more. She's a working mom, and she's often tired. I'm going to clean my room and take the dog out every day…and wash the dishes in the evenings!

Tony Soto (31)
Chico, California
I spend too much time on my computer. I have lots of friends on the Internet but no friends in my life! So I'm going to try a dating service…and make some new friends.

What is she/he going to do?		
Liana	Amy	Tony
1. get more exercise	**1.**	**1.**
2.	**2.**	**2.**
3.	**3.**	
	4.	

B. Read the article again. Write **T** (true) or **F** (false).

1. ___F___ Liana is a student.

2. _____ Now, Liana takes the bus every day.

3. _____ Now, Amy helps her mom a lot.

4. _____ Amy often washes the dishes now.

5. _____ Tony has a girlfriend.

① *Going to:* Statements

Look at the picture. What is going to happen? Write seven sentences. Use one of these words in each sentence.

backache	**deliver**	**miss**	**rain**
~~**book**~~	**eat out**	**photograph**	**turn**

Example: Agnes is going to buy a book.

1. _____

2. _____

3. _____

4. _____

5. _____

6. _____

7. _____

❷ A Computer Dating Interview

Linda is at a computer dating service. Read the interview. Then write the questions that are missing.

1. Q: _What's your name?_

A: Linda Kensington.

2. Q: _____

A: Nineteen.

3. Q: _____

A: I'm a business student, and I work part-time.

4. Q: _____

A: At a bookstore near my home.

5. Q: _____

A: Well, I don't have a lot of free time, but I like to swim, go to movies, listen to music . . .

SUPER Challenge

❸ Power Writing: An Interview

Now write a conversation between you and an interviewer. Use the conversation in Exercise 2 as a guide.

A: _____

B: _____

A: _____

B: _____

A: _____

B: _____

A: _____

B: _____

Unit 7 Can you dance?

❶ Write about yourself.

Write sentences with **I have to** or **I don't have to**.

> **Examples:** get up early <u>I have to get up early.</u>
>
> go to work <u>I don't have to go to work.</u>

uniform

1. study for exams _____

2. buy food for my family _____

3. speak English in class _____

4. wear a uniform every day _____

5. do homework _____

6. work on the weekend _____

❷ Write sentences.

Mike is having a party tonight. But nobody can come!
Write sentences with **have, has, have to,** or **has to**.

1. Tom / headache <u>Tom has a headache.</u>

2. Melissa / study for a test <u>Melissa has to study for a test.</u>

3. Amy / work late tonight _____

4. Trisha / sore throat _____

5. Carl and Pete / do homework _____

6. Thomas and Alicia / date _____

7. Leroy / fever _____

8. Keiko / help her mother _____

3 Write answers.

A. *Tell about yourself. Use short answers.*

(Can you cross your eyes?)

> **Example:** Can you drive? _____No, I can't._____

1. Can you sing well? _____

2. Can you cook? _____

3. Can you cross your eyes? _____

B. *Now write some sentences about yourself.*

> **Example:** _____I can't dance well._____

1. _____

2. _____

3. _____

Challenge

4 Read and answer questions.

Read the text and answer the questions about the United States.

> In the United States, all children have to go to school from age six to age sixteen. Some schools, especially private schools, have uniforms, but most public schools do not. When they finish high school, American teenagers get a high school diploma. If they want to go to college they have to take the SAT exam.
>
> In the United States you can vote and get married at age eighteen and drive a car at age fifteen or sixteen. You have to take a test before you can get a driver's license.

1. At what age do children have to go to school? _____Six._____

2. Do all students have to wear uniforms at school? _____No._____

3. Do all students have to take an examination when they finish high school? _____

4. At what age can you get married? _____

5. At what age can you drive a car? _____

⑤ Read and match.

A. Who wrote the invitations? Write a letter below each invitation.

a.   b.   c.   d.

To: Becky

    Come to my birthday party!

When: Saturday August 14, 3 P.M.

Where: 1164 Moncada Drive

    RSVP

1. ___c___

Dear Mary,
    There's a dance at the Senior Club on Wednesday. I need a partner, and I know you like to waltz. Can you come with me?
Regards,

2. _____

Memo

Tony:
How about a game of tennis tonight? We can meet at my office at 6:00 P.M.

3. _____

Hi Jody—
Let's go to Rock City tonight! There's a new band playing, and it's free!

4. _____

B. *Read the replies. Write the number of the correct invitation under each reply.*

JIM:
I CAN'T MEET AT 6 P.M.
BUT WHAT ABOUT LATER?
6:30? I'D LOVE A GAME.

Hi CARY,
SORRY BUT I CAN'T.
I HAVE TO STAY
HOME TONIGHT TO
HELP MY MOM.
WHAT A BUMMER.

a. invitation number: _____3_____

b. invitation number: _____

Dear Edward,
Thank you so much
for inviting me!
I can't dance
very well, but I'd
love to go to the
dance with you.

Dear Susie,
I can come
to your
party.
Love,

c. invitation number: _____

d. invitation number: _____

⑥ Unscramble the conversation.

Put the conversation in the correct order.

_____ I am. This chemistry homework is really hard. Can you help me?

_____ Well, can you help me later?

_____ Sure.

___1___ What's the matter? You look worried.

_____ Yes, but not now. I have to wash my hair.

_____ Thanks a million.

7 Read and make a list.

Read the article.

Whiz in a Wheelchair

He can't walk, but he can move pretty fast in his wheelchair, and he's training to go even faster. Fifteen-year-old James Parker is a table tennis champion, and he likes wheelchair racing, too!

James was in a bad car accident at the age of six. Now he cannot use his legs, and he has to use a wheelchair. James "drives" the chair with his arms. He also plays video games, and in the summer he plays basketball with his brothers.

But his favorite place is at the table tennis (Ping-Pong) table. James practices every day for an hour after school. "I want to win a gold medal," he says. "I'm sure I can do it. And I want other kids like me to think that they can win, too."

James's house has a special ramp so that he can go in and out of the house easily. At Adams High School in Champaign, Illinois, James is a popular student. He works hard, although he has to sit at the back of the classroom because of his chair. He doesn't mind that at all. "I like it back there," he says. "The teachers can't see me."

a champion

a wheelchair

a car accident

a Ping-Pong table

Now write a list of things that James can do.

a medal

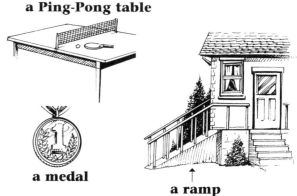

a ramp

1.   He can move pretty fast in his wheelchair. _____

2. _____

3. _____

4. _____

5. _____

POWER ACTIVITIES

① Vocabulary Power

A. *Fill in the missing verbs.*

1. __make__ pizza

2. _____ guitar

3. _____ Spanish

4. _____ magic tricks

5. _____ a song

6. _____ a truck

7. _____ basketball

8. _____ the waltz

B. *Which of the activities can you do? Which ones can't you do? Write two sentences.*

Example: ‥‥‥‥ _I can make pizza. I can't play the guitar._____

_____

_____

② Auxiliary Verbs

*Fill in the blanks with **can, can't, do, don't, have to,** or **has to.***

A: Penny? It's Lydia. Listen. There's a jazz concert tonight at 9 o'clock. ____Do____ you
1.
want to come?

B: Maybe. I _____ know. What time is it at?
2.

A: It's at nine. But I'm outside the theater right now, so I _____ get the tickets if
3.
you like.

B: Oh, Lydia. I _____ study. I have a test tomorrow, remember?
4.

A: I know! But it's only five o'clock now. You _____ study until eight-thirty.
5.

B: Why _____ you call Thomas? He likes jazz.
6.

A: He _____ come. He _____ babysit.
7.   **8.**

B: OK, tell you what. I _____ be there at nine fifteen. _____ you wait for me?
9.   **10.**

A: Sure! I'll see you then.

❸ Power Writing: A Conversation

Look at the picture. What do you think the people are saying? Complete the conversation.

A: _Ted? It's Carla. I'm going to see "The Forgotten" tonight. Do you want to come?_

B: _____

A: _____

B: _____

A: _____

B: _____

A: _____

B: _____

A: _____

B: _____

Do you want some pizza, Lulu?

1 Unscramble the conversation.

Put the conversation in the correct order.

_____	Forty dollars.
_____	Yes? How can I help you?
_____	Do you have any jackets?
___1___	Excuse me.
_____	This red one is nice. How much is it?
_____	Forty dollars? I'll take it.
_____	Sure. Follow me.

2 Complete the sentences.

*Fill in the blanks with **some** or **any**.*

1. I need ____some____ shoes.

2. I don't have ____any____ money.

3. I want _____ ice cream.

4. There isn't _____ pizza left.

5. There are _____ good restaurants on Clay Street.

6. There's _____ water on the table.

7. Michael doesn't have _____ brothers or sisters.

8. Please give me _____ information.

9. There aren't _____ good movies at this theater.

10. We don't have _____ homework tonight.

11. She wants _____ coffee.

12. Sorry, I don't have _____ money.

❸ Find the words.

Todd is talking to his friend.
Read what he says. Then draw arrows
*to the words **one** and **ones** refer to.*

"It's my birthday tomorrow. I'm going
to be ten. And I'm going to get some presents!
I hope my grandma gives me some running
shoes. The **ones** I have are too small. And
I want black **ones.**

"And I'm getting a science computer game like the **one** that Mario has. It's a really
good **one.** But you have to go to a special store. The **one** in Glenwood is pretty good.
It's a special **one** just for computer games."

❹ Complete the conversations.

Fill in the blanks.

1. **A:** I need _____an_____ umbrella. Do you have umbrellas?

   B: Sure. Right this way.

   A: I like this black _____one_____. How much is _____?

   B: Twelve dollars.

   A: OK, I'll take _____.

2. **A:** I need _____ socks. Do you sell socks?

   B: Sure. Right this way.

   A: I like these blue _____. How much are _____?

   B: Seven dollars.

   A: OK, I'll take _____.

5 Write vocabulary words.

Label the clothes in the picture. Use the words in the box.

pants
sweater
~~shirt~~
glove
socks
boots
skirt
belt
blouse
panty hose
shoes
raincoat

1. *shirt*
2.
3.
4.
5.
6.

7.
8.
9.
10.
11.
12.

6 Circle the word.

Circle the word that does not belong.

1. nightgown   pajamas   (gloves)

2. skirt   (baseball cap)   dress

3. socks   mittens   gloves

4. shoes   shorts   socks

5. dress   raincoat   umbrella

6. briefs   undershirt   belt

7. bra   suit   panties

8. sport shirt   mittens   dress shirt

9. nightgown   boots   sandals

10. underwear   boxer shorts   coat

❼ Write about yourself.

Answer the questions. Use short answers.

<u>**Example:**</u>   Do you have a pair of sandals?   <u>Yes, I do.</u>

1. What size shoes do you wear?   _____

2. Do you often wear running shoes?   _____

3. Are you wearing a sweater right now?   _____

4. Do you have an umbrella?   _____

5. Do you have a baseball cap?   _____

6. Do you have to wear a tie to work?   _____

7. Are you wearing a belt right now?   _____

8. Do you wear gloves in the winter?   _____

❽ Rewrite sentences.

Challenge

A. *Rewrite each sentence, making the underlined words and phrases* **plural***.*

1. I have <u>a problem</u>.   <u>I have some problems.</u>

2. Is that your <u>CD</u>?   <u>Are those your CDs?</u>

3. He wants <u>a tie</u> for his birthday.   _____

4. There's <u>an umbrella</u> over there.   _____

5. There isn't <u>a doctor</u> here.   _____

6. Do you have that <u>book</u>?   _____

B. *Now rewrite these sentences, making the underlined words and phrases* **singular***.*

1. I love those <u>sweaters</u>.   <u>I love that sweater.</u>

2. Those <u>T-shirts</u> are the large ones.   <u>That T-shirt is the large one.</u>

3. Those <u>books</u> are very good.   _____

4. She wants some <u>CDs</u>.   _____

5. These <u>movies</u> aren't interesting.   _____

6. <u>They</u> are good ones.   _____

Read the article. Then write the correct name under each picture.

Teens Talk about Style

···

With so many different "looks" to choose from nowadays, today's teens can choose the look they like best. And it doesn't have to cost a lot of money. We asked four teenagers to give us their views on fashion.

Rebecca (16)

I think it's important to be comfortable. I shop at thrift stores, where you can find lots of really cheap clothes. Then I mix and match. I wear big shirts with skirts, or old jeans with a pretty blouse. I like to be comfortable. It's stupid to pay $100 for a pair of jeans.

Don (14)

I wear shorts all year because they're comfortable. I live in San Diego, so it doesn't get very cold. My parents are OK about it. Kids in school think it's normal. I almost never wear a suit.

Jess (15)

I like to wear casual clothes: pants and sports shirts, usually. I have a blue jacket. I wear it everywhere. My brother wears really big pants. I hate that. I think it looks stupid. Girls don't like it either.

April (17)

I like black. Everything I have is black. I wear black pants and sweaters, or a black dress and boots. I even have black pajamas that my mom gave me for Christmas. They're so cool! I have a lot of different jewelry, too.

···

1. ___Don___   **2.** _____   **3.** _____   **4.** _____

POWER ACTIVITIES

❶ A, An, or Some?

*Write **a**, **an**, or **some**.*

1. ___a___ book
2. ___an___ umbrella
3. ___some___ money
4. _____ jacket
5. _____ water
6. _____ T-shirts

7. _____ restaurant
8. _____ help
9. _____ ties
10. _____ milk
11. _____ undershirt
12. _____ pants

❷ Questions and Answers

Match the questions with the answers.

1. ___c___ Which dress do you like?
2. _____ Do you have a bathroom?
3. _____ Do you like these boots?
4. _____ How much is that T-shirt?
5. _____ Do you like that jacket over there?
6. _____ What size do you wear?
7. _____ Do you have any baseball caps?
8. _____ How much are the running shoes?
9. _____ Which pants do you want?
10. _____ Where are the umbrellas?

a. I'll take the black ones.
b. It's $12.99.
c. The blue one.
d. Medium.
e. No. We don't have any right now.
f. They're $65.
g. They're over there.
h. Yes, but it's expensive!
i. Yes. There's one on the second floor.
j. Yes. They're very nice.

❸ Find the Mistakes

Correct the mistake(s) in each sentence.

1. Excuse me. I need ~~any~~ *a* new tie.

2. I usually wear a pants to work.

3. I like this blue sandals.

4. Sorry, we don't have an umbrellas.

5. That jacket is nice. How much are they?

6. There's a blue jeans over there.

7. Do you like these sweater?

8. Can I see that socks, please?

❹ Power Writing: A Conversation

Look at the picture. Write the conversation that the people are having. Include some of these phrases.

I need	what size	do you like	do you have	how much	over there

_____

_____

_____

_____

_____

_____

_____

Weren't you at Alice's?

❶ Rewrite sentences.

Rewrite each sentence in the past tense.

1. It's a beautiful day.   _It was a beautiful day._

2. That's my boss.   _____

3. We're not at home.   _____

4. There's a party on Saturday.   _____

5. She's not at work.   _____

6. That sweater isn't very nice.   _____

7. There are twelve students in my class.   _____

8. You're late.   _____

9. He's a good swimmer.   _____

❷ Write about yourself.

Answer the questions. Use short answers.

Example: Were you in class yesterday?   _Yes, I was. or No, I wasn't._

1. Were you at home the day before yesterday?   _____

2. Was it cold in your city yesterday?   _____

3. Were you at a party last weekend?   _____

4. Were you hungry this morning?   _____

5. Was there an English test last week?   _____

❸ Complete the conversation.

Complete the conversation between a boy and his mother.
Use words from the box. Use the words more than once.

was	wasn't	were	weren't

A: Look at this photo, Mom! Is that you?

B: Sure it is.

A: Where was that?

B: That _____was_____ in Africa.
   1.

A: Africa? When _____were_____ you in Africa?
   2.

B: In 1974 and 1975.

A: _____ Dad there, too?
   3.

B: No, he _____.
   4.

A: Wow! _____ it hot there?
   5.

B: Yes, it _____. Hot and wet. But it _____ great.
   6.   **7.**

A: Who are those people in the picture?

B: Well, let me see. That guy. . .his name _____ David. He _____
   8.   **9.**

   my boss at the time. We _____ both in the same town.
   10.

A: And who are those people?

B: They _____ our neighbors. We _____ friends with them.
   11.   **12.**

A: And this guy? Who's that?

B: His name _____ Paul. He _____ my boyfriend.
   13.   **14.**

A: Your boyfriend? But where _____ Dad?
   15.

B: Dad and I _____ married then.
   16.

4 Complete the sentences.

Fill in the blanks. Use words from the box.

assistant	boss
fiancé(e)	neighbors
partner	roommate

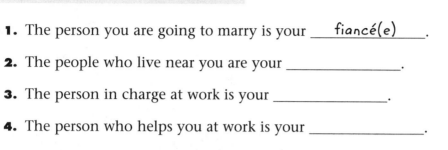

1. The person you are going to marry is your ___fiancé(e)___.

2. The people who live near you are your _____.

3. The person in charge at work is your _____.

4. The person who helps you at work is your _____.

5. The person who lives in an apartment with you is your _____.

6. The person who owns your business with you is your _____.

Challenge

5 Unscramble the conversation.

Put the conversation in the correct order.

_____ At home. Why?

___1___ Jenny, where were you last night?

_____ Jason.

_____ There was a party at Anita's house.

_____ Yes. He was gorgeous!

_____ Kate and Jordan...and some of Anita's friends from work...and there was a really nice guy from the university.

_____ I know. He was my boyfriend last year!

_____ Oh, yeah? What was his name?

_____ Really? Who was there?

_____ Jason? Was he tall, with blond hair?

6 Complete the conversations.

*Write the questions. Use **was** and **were**.*

1. A: (Where / you last night?) ___Where were you last night?___

   B: I was at a movie.

2. A: (Who / in it?) _____

   B: Michelle Pfeiffer and Brad Pitt.

3. A: Sounds good. (it / a love story?) _____

   B: No, actually, it was a comedy.

4. A: (Who / with you?) _____

   B: Just some friends. Oh, yes! There was a woman from Boston there. She knows you.

5. A: Really? (What / her name?) _____

   B: Judy.

6. A: Judy? (tall, with glasses?) _____

   B: Wow! She was my roommate in college.

7 Choose the correct word.

Circle the correct word.

1. Those shoes are (my / (mine)).

2. John, where's ((your) / yours) book?

3. (My / Mine) mother works at the supermarket.

4. Give that sweater to Charlie. It's (his / hers).

5. Is that (your / yours) house? It's very big!

6. No, this one is (our / ours).

7. Children, come on in! (Your / Yours) dinner is ready.

8. Jeff and Rick are (our / ours) neighbors.

9. Whose shoes are these? Are they (your / yours), Kate?

10. That bike is (my / mine).

11. Our computer isn't the same as (their / theirs).

8 Read and find differences.

*Look at the picture. Then read the text. Find five differences between the text and the picture.
Circle them.*

I remember my grandmother's living room well. There was a big sofa, and there were (two) comfortable chairs. It was quite dark, because there was only one window. And there were a lot of plants. There was an old piano in one corner of the room. A photo of my grandfather as a young man was on the piano. My grandfather was so handsome! There were other photos on the wall, and I think there was a big picture of the ocean. There was a bookcase full of books, and a clock on the bookcase. But the clock was broken: It was always five o'clock!

POWER ACTIVITIES

❶ Possessive Pronouns

Write the correct expression for each picture. Two expressions will not be used.

Are these yours?	**It's theirs.**	**This is hers.**
Is this his?	**That's mine.**	**Those are ours.**

1. _____

2. _____

3. _____

4. _____

❷ *Was* and *Were: Wh-* Questions

Make questions for the underlined answers.

1. I was <u>at home</u> last night.   *Where were you last night?* _____

2. The concert was <u>in the afternoon</u>. _____

3. <u>Mark</u> was with me. _____

4. My neighbor's name was <u>Cindy</u>. _____

5. We were late <u>because of the weather</u>. _____

6. Madeline and Tim were <u>in Paris</u>. _____

7. I was in London <u>in 2001</u>. _____

8. The party was <u>at Gail's house</u>. _____

3 A Quiz

Which questions can you answer? Choose from the answers in the box below. Use **was** *and* **were**.

a singer	an actress	the Beatles
a painter	a writer	Barcelona, Spain

1. Who was Elvis Presley?   *He was a singer.*

2. Who was Agatha Christie?   _____

3. Who was Marilyn Monroe?   _____

4. Who was Diego Rivera?   _____

5. Who were John, Paul, George, and Ringo?   _____

6. Where were the Olympic games in 1992?   _____

SUPER Challenge

4 Power Writing: A Room I Remember

A. *Think about a room that you remember well from the past. Answer the questions.*

What kind of room was it (big, small, dark, bright, modern, comfortable)?

_____

What kind of furniture was there (a bed, a sofa, chairs, a table, windows, a television)?

_____

What other things were there (pictures, books, magazines, plants, a clock)?

_____

B. *Now write a paragraph describing the room. Use the description on Workbook page 50 as an example.*

_____

_____

_____

_____

Unit 10 — My plane just landed.

❶ Write the verbs.

A. *Write the simple past tense form of these verbs.*

1. do ___did___
2. come _____
3. take _____
4. feel _____
5. play _____

6. go _____
7. say _____
8. call _____
9. meet _____
10. make _____

11. tell _____
12. get _____
13. find _____
14. see _____
15. hear _____

B. *Now fill in the blanks. Use the simple past tense forms above. Use each verb only once.*

1. I ___took___ the bus to work this morning.

2. Evan _____ the police when he saw the accident.

3. We _____ to Hawaii on vacation last year.

4. I _____ my homework at five o'clock.

5. I _____ my wife for the first time when we were in college.

6. "Come over here!" she _____.

7. We _____ basketball for two hours last night.

8. I _____ that movie last week.

9. My grandparents _____ to this country from Japan.

10. My brother _____ this sweater in Ireland.

11. I lost my watch, but I _____ it today.

12. When my grandfather died, I _____ very sad.

13. We stayed home last night, and my mom _____ pizza.

14. I _____ Beth about the party, but she didn't go.

15. We _____ beautiful music coming from my son's room.

❷ Write words and sentences.

A. Fill in the blanks. Use the words from the box.

CDs	cars	computers	phone	plane	movies	supermarkets	TV

It's the end of the 20th century, and our lives are fast. People drive _____*cars*_____.
                                                                                1.

We travel around the world by _____. We use _____ at work, and
                                                    2.   3.

we shop in _____. We don't write letters very much. Instead, we talk on the
                          4.

_____. For entertainment, we don't play music or tell stories: We go to
              5.

_____, watch _____, and listen to _____.
            6.   7.   8.

B. Now write negative sentences.

Three hundred years ago, life was different. In 1700,

1. cars _____People didn't drive cars._____

2. plane _____People didn't travel around the world by plane._____

3. computers _____

4. supermarkets _____

5. phone _____

6. movies _____

7. TV _____

8. CDs _____

52   UNIT 10

❸ Write questions and answers.

*Write **did** or **were.** Then answer the questions. Tell about yourself.*

Example: ___Did___ you get up early this morning?   ___No, I didn't.___

___Were___ you at home last night?   ___Yes, I was.___

1. _____ you at school today?   _____

2. _____ you watch TV last night?   _____

3. _____ you on vacation last month?   _____

4. _____ you have coffee this morning?   _____

5. _____ you go to the supermarket yesterday?   _____

❹ Match beginnings and endings.

Look at the calendar. Then finish the sentences.

May						
Sunday	Monday	Tuesday	Wednesday	Thursday	Friday	Saturday
				1	2	3
4	5	6	7	8	9	10
11	12	13	(14)	15	16	17
18	19	20	21	22		4
25	30					

Today is Wednesday, May 14th.

1. ___f___ May 13th was   **a.** last month.

2. _____ May 8th was   **b.** last week.

3. _____ May 12th was   **c.** a few days ago.

4. _____ April was   **d.** the day before yesterday.

5. _____ May 4th–10th was   **e.** last Thursday.

6. _____ May 11th was   **f.** yesterday.

5 Unscramble the conversation.

A. *Put the conversation in the correct order.*

_____ Sounds like fun. I love tennis. How was the food?

_____ What did you do?

_____ Yesterday morning.

___1___ Hi, Jim! When did you get back?

_____ We played tennis, and we went swimming every day.

_____ So how was Hawaii?

_____ Terrific!

_____ We did! We're going to go back again next year.

_____ Delicious! We had fresh fish every day.

_____ Sounds like you had a great time.

B. *Now write the questions for these answers.*

1. A: _Hi! When did you get back?_____

B: Last night.

2. A: _____ New York?

B: It was great. We had a wonderful time.

3. A: _____?

B: Oh, the usual tourist things . . . we saw the

Empire State Building, and we went to Broadway, and we saw a play. . . .

4. A: _____?

B: Delicious, of course. But the restaurants were pretty expensive.

5. A: _____ weather?

B: Cold and rainy! But we had a good time anyway.

6 Read and answer questions.

A. *Read about Brad Pitt. As you read, look for the answers to these questions.*

1. Where was he born? _____

2. Did he graduate from college? _____

3. What movie began his career? _____

4. How much money does he make for one movie now? _____

5. Does he like to give interviews? _____

William Bradley ("Brad") Pitt was born in Oklahoma. He was the oldest of three children. He went to Kickapoo High School, where he was a good student. After high school, he went to the University of Missouri to study journalism.

But Brad didn't really want to be a journalist; he wanted to act in movies. So, two weeks before college graduation, he got in his car and drove to Hollywood.

Success did not come immediately. For several years, Brad did odd jobs to make money. In one job, for a fast-food restaurant, he dressed up as a giant chicken! Like many other young actors, he also worked as a chauffeur, driving limousines around Los Angeles. In his free time, he took acting classes.

Finally, at age 25, Brad got the role he needed: He was "JD" in the movie *Thelma and Louise.* This helped him start his new career. Other movies, such as *Legends of the Fall* and *Twelve Monkeys,* soon followed. Now he's one of the hottest young stars in Hollywood. He's famous for his good looks. He can get 8 million dollars for one movie.

In real life, Pitt is a private person. He gives very few interviews. "I don't know anything about my favorite actors," he once told an interviewer. "And I don't want people to know about me."

B. *Find a word or phrase in the text which means:*

1. low-paid, part-time work (paragraph 3): _____

2. very large (paragraph 3): _____

3. a person who drives people's cars (paragraph 3): _____

4. large expensive cars (paragraph 3): _____

5. the character an actor plays in a movie (paragraph 4): _____

6. famous movie actors or singers (paragraph 4): _____

POWER ACTIVITIES

1 Simple Past Forms

A. Fill in the blanks with the simple past forms of the verbs.

Meryl Streep ____was____ born in 1949, and _____ up in a wealthy area
  1. be   2. grow
of New Jersey. She _____ acting in high school. She _____
                     3. start   4. get
a scholarship to the Yale School of Drama, and _____ in 1975.
                                                 5. graduate

After graduating, Streep _____ to New York City and
                          6. move
_____ in the theater. In 1977, she _____ her first
 7. work   8. make
movie, *Julia*, with Jane Fonda and Vanessa Redgrave. She
_____ her first Oscar in 1979, for *Kramer vs Kramer*.
 9. get

By then, Streep _____ one of the most promising young actresses in
                  10. be
Hollywood. She _____ on to act in many movies, including *Sophie's Choice*, *Out of*
                11. go
Africa, and *The Hours*. In 2002, Streep _____ a magazine writer in *Adaptation*, earning
                                            12. play
her 13th Oscar nomination. She is now the most-nominated actor in the history of Hollywood.

Streep _____ a sculptor, Don Gummer, in 1978. The couple lives in
        13. marry
Connecticut with their four children.

B. Now write questions for these answers.

1. In 1949.   When was Meryl Streep born? _____

2. In New Jersey.   _____

3. In 1975.   _____

4. *Julia*.   _____

5. 1979.   _____

6. Don Gummer.   _____

❷ A Vacation

Fill in the blanks with the simple past, affirmative, or negative form of one of the words below. If necessary, refer to the list of irregular verbs on page 150 of your Student Book. Try to use all of the words. You may use some more than once.

be	have	buy	~~get~~	see	wait	go	take

I just _____got_____ back from a week in London! We _____ a great time. There
      1.   **2.**

_____ only one problem: the hotel _____ very good.
3.   **4.**

We _____ two shows, "Hats" and "The Tiger Queen." They _____
     5.   **6.**

fantastic! We _____ to the Tower of London too. We _____ in line for an hour to
          7.   **8.**

get in, but it _____ very interesting and we _____ lots of photos. We _____
          9.   **10.**   **11.**

shopping too, but we _____ a lot, because things _____ very expensive.
                    12.   **13.**

SUPER Challenge

❸ Power Writing: On my vacation, . . .

Think about a vacation you took recently (or use the pictures to imagine a vacation). Where did you go and when? Who did you go with? How long did you stay? Where did you stay? What did you do? Did you have a good time? Why or why not? Write a paragraph describing the vacation you took (or imagined).

_____

_____

_____

_____

_____

_____

❶ Fill in the blanks.

Fill in the blanks. Use words from the box. Use some words more than once.

do	go	have	make	am	watch	need

1. Do you want to _____*go*_____ to a movie on Saturday?

2. I'm going home. I have to _____ my homework.

3. My husband and I usually _____ dinner at five o'clock and eat at six o'clock.

4. We're going to _____ swimming.

5. I can't work today. I _____ a fever.

6. She can't come. She has to _____ to dance class.

7. I _____ an appointment with the doctor. I _____ a backache.

8. Do you want to _____ biking this afternoon?

9. I think I'm sick. I _____ dizzy.

10. Let's _____ TV tonight.

❷ Unscramble the sentences.

Write sentences. The first word is capitalized.

1. at / at / o'clock / He / ten / is / usually / work

_____He is usually at work at ten o'clock._____

2. a / in / July / takes / She / usually / vacation

_____

3. a / every / have / I / day / to / wear / uniform

_____

4. a / evening / father / headache / My / has / often / in / the

_____

❸ Match beginnings and endings.

Match the expressions on the left with the correct responses on the right.

1. ___e___   Where were you last night?   **a.** That's OK. I'm not mad at you.

2. _____   I'm busy now, but I can help   **b.** So do you. Weren't you at Kate's
             you later.   party last night?

3. _____   I'm really sorry about that.   **c.** No, that's not fair. Let's go Dutch.

4. _____   How about eleven o'clock?   **d.** Seven dollars.

5. _____   I like these. How much are they?   **e.** At home. Why?

6. _____   What's the matter? You look worried.   **f.** Thanks a million.

7. _____   It's my turn to pay.   **g.** Laura and I were in school together.

8. _____   How do you know Laura?   **h.** I am. This homework is really hard.

9. _____   You look familiar.   **i.** That's a little difficult. I'm going to
                                                            be in class until twelve.

❹ Complete the puzzle.

Write the simple past tense forms of the verbs in the blanks, and find a mystery word!

1. come
2. get
3. go
4. forget
5. hear
6. have
7. take
8. find
9. feel
10. say
11. meet
12. do
13. tell
14. know
15. see

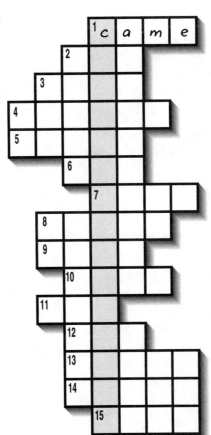

The mystery word is _____.

5 Write questions and answers.

A. *Read the letter. As you read, look for the answers to these questions.*

1. Who is the letter from? _____

2. Where is she? _____

3. Who is the letter to? (Hint: Look at the last paragraph.) _____

Hi there, guys!

    We're having a great time in California. We're staying with my sister Monica, (the one who's a journalist) in her wonderful house in Beverly Hills! So we're living in style. Monica's at work most of the time, so we can just lie around the pool or play tennis. The weather is wonderful, of course!

    We're going to all the new movies because Monica has to write about them. (Terrible, huh?) Everybody in Hollywood talks about movies all the time. And last week we took a tour around Beverly Hills and saw all the homes of the stars. (Wow!) Then on Saturday we went to Universal Studios. And who do you think we saw? Jack Nicholson! Monica knows him, so she introduced us to him, and he was so nice!

    And of course the food is great. Every evening Monica takes us to a new restaurant to try Thai food, Japanese food, Korean food . . . a different kind every night. It's all good.

    Anyway, I have to go now. Tom and I are going to swim before dinner. I never want to go back to Kansas — or back to work! But I guess I have to! See you all at work next week.

Lots of love,
Kim

B. *Now make questions for the following answers.*

Questions	Answers
1. Who _is the letter from?_	Kim.
2. Where _____	With her sister Monica.
3. Where _____	They went to Universal Studios.
4. Who _____	Jack Nicholson.
5. What _____	She's going to go back to work.

TEST-TAKING SKILLS

SECTION I
Vocabulary You Should Know

> 1. Read the sentence(s).
> 2. Try each answer in the space.
> 3. Circle the letter of the answer that best completes the sentence.

1. Where are you _____? We have to be at the party in fifteen minutes!

   (A) getting
   (B) leaving
   (C) worrying
   (D) going

2. You look sick. Why don't you make _____ with the doctor?

   (A) an appointment
   (B) a problem
   (C) an office
   (D) an apartment

3. I'm going to a business _____. It's at an office downtown.

   (A) meeting
   (B) date
   (C) work
   (D) time

4. Jerry has a sore _____, but he has to go to work.

   (A) soccer
   (B) talking
   (C) throat
   (D) dance

5. _____ is good exercise, but you need a good partner to tango.

   (A) Studying
   (B) Dancing
   (C) Fishing
   (D) Watching TV

6. _____ is a difficult class. There is homework every night.

   (A) Clothing
   (B) Character
   (C) Chemistry
   (D) Cough

7. I don't usually wear _____ on a day like today. It's too warm.

   (A) a sweater
   (B) sandals
   (C) an umbrella
   (D) a bathing suit

8. Clothes are expensive. I saw a pair of _____ for two hundred dollars.

   (A) sleepwear
   (B) belts
   (C) skirts
   (D) pants

9. What _____ suit do you wear?

   (A) sandals
   (B) shorts
   (C) size
   (D) sweater

10. Excuse me. Can you _____ me? I need a new tie.

    (A) help
    (B) pay
    (C) find
    (D) get

11. Her boyfriend is _____ from the military. He came home last week.

   (A) later
   (B) back
   (C) rarely
   (D) earlier

12. I have two _____. We have a nice apartment.

   (A) patients
   (B) assistants
   (C) roommates
   (D) bosses

13. Jason has a lot of problems with his boss. He is _____ about his job.

   (A) excited
   (B) worried
   (C) dizzy
   (D) bored

14. I forgot my book at home. Can I use _____, Bill?

   (A) ours
   (B) yours
   (C) mine
   (D) hers

15. Gracie _____ her cousin for the first time a few days ago. Now they are good friends.

   (A) said
   (B) knew
   (C) forgot
   (D) met

SECTION 2
Vocabulary from Context

> 1. Read the sentence(s).
> 2. Try each answer in place of the underlined word(s).
> 3. Circle the letter of the best answer.

1. My legs are sore from running. I played soccer for four hours yesterday.

   (A) hurt
   (B) exercise
   (C) practice
   (D) feel

2. Margie is thrilled about the party. All of her friends are coming.

   (A) hard
   (B) bored
   (C) excited
   (D) dizzy

3. She frequently swims in the morning. She goes five days a week.

   (A) later
   (B) often
   (C) earlier
   (D) well

4. He is wearing a navy blazer with his yellow shirt and tie. He also has on gray pants.

   (A) jacket
   (B) bathing suit
   (C) nightgown
   (D) blouse

5. Leo is a new teacher, and he is apprehensive. He's worried about his new job.

    (A) familiar
    (B) funny
    (C) easy
    (D) nervous

6. Excuse me. Can you please assist me? I need a different size.

    (A) look
    (B) hear
    (C) help
    (D) find

7. I can see a couple of cats in the snow. There are only two, I think.

    (A) pair
    (B) twin
    (C) size
    (D) meeting

8. Rick has a new helper at the office. She answers the phone and takes messages for him.

    (A) boss
    (B) assistant
    (C) neighbor
    (D) partner

9. Jane sells nightclothes. Her department has pajamas, nightgowns, and slippers in all sizes.

    (A) underwear
    (B) sport shirts
    (C) bathing suits
    (D) sleepwear

10. She likes to work out early in the morning. There aren't many people in the gym at that hour.

    (A) exercise
    (B) dance
    (C) study
    (D) hike

11. Jane is married, but I don't know her spouse's name.

    (A) father's
    (B) son's
    (C) husband's
    (D) brother's

12. You resemble your grandmother. You have the same eyes and mouth.

    (A) walk like
    (B) look like
    (C) talk like
    (D) dance like

13. Sandy works Monday through Friday. She doesn't work Saturday or Sunday.

    (A) a few days ago
    (B) weekends
    (C) evenings
    (D) weekdays

14. The farmers planted coffee and bananas together.

    (A) worked
    (B) took
    (C) grew
    (D) saw

15. I'm exhausted. I studied for my test until 3:00 in the morning.

    (A) bored
    (B) dizzy
    (C) tired
    (D) familiar

SECTION 3
Sentence Structure

> 1. Read the sentence(s).
> 2. Try each answer in the space.
> 3. Circle the letter of the answer that best completes the sentence.

1. He _____ his girlfriend yesterday.
   - (A) is calling
   - (B) called
   - (C) calls
   - (D) calling

2. The store doesn't have _____ blue shoes in my size.
   - (A) any
   - (B) no
   - (C) much
   - (D) this

3. Where _____ the students going to play volleyball?
   - (A) are
   - (B) they are playing
   - (C) isn't she playing
   - (D) they're going to

4. Do you _____, baseball, swimming, or soccer?
   - (A) have games
   - (B) playing
   - (C) like basketball
   - (D) in the summer

5. I _____ you some dance steps right now.
   - (A) teaching
   - (B) am I teaching
   - (C) can teach
   - (D) a teacher

6. _____ going to like calculus class this semester.
   - (A) Is
   - (B) They
   - (C) Why
   - (D) You're

7. How can I _____ you?
   - (A) help
   - (B) helping
   - (C) helped
   - (D) helps

8. My friends opened a clothing store downtown _____.
   - (A) they
   - (B) in the
   - (C) last month
   - (D) are opening

9. What size shirt does _____?
   - (A) he wears
   - (B) he wear
   - (C) he is wearing
   - (D) is he wearing

10. Is that red sweater his, or is it _____?
    - (A) her
    - (B) our
    - (C) mine
    - (D) your

11. The _____ don't like rock music.

    (A) neighbors
    (B) man
    (C) boy's mother
    (D) woman's boss

12. Your voice sounds _____. Are you Amy's husband?

    (A) sometimes
    (B) hers
    (C) heard
    (D) familiar

13. The _____ over there are nice.

    (A) your
    (B) ones
    (C) that
    (D) one

14. The two little boys _____ the piano every day.

    (A) playing
    (B) on
    (C) practiced
    (D) to listen to

15. The children _____ good athletes, and their mother was proud of them.

    (A) he was
    (B) were
    (C) they all
    (D) was from

SECTION 4
Error Correction

> 1. Read the sentence.
> 2. Read the underlined words and the words around them.
> 3. Circle the letter below the word that is <u>not</u> correct.

1. Today <u>people</u> are <u>worries</u> about money, <u>family</u>, and <u>work</u>.
          A   B   C   D

2. Whose <u>shoes</u> <u>are</u> <u>these</u>? Are they <u>your</u>?
          A   B   C   D

3. People <u>usually</u> <u>wearing</u> warm <u>clothes</u> in the <u>winter</u>.
           A   B   C   D

4. Rose <u>lost</u> <u>her</u> jacket <u>yesterday</u>, but she <u>find</u> it today.
         A B   C   D

5. Sheila didn't <u>knew</u> the people <u>at</u> the party, so she <u>didn't</u> talk to <u>them</u>.
              A   B   C   D

6. Many <u>students</u> don't <u>have</u> <u>some</u> free <u>time</u> on weekdays.
            A   B   C   D

7. I <u>can't</u> <u>coming</u> to the <u>party</u> <u>on</u> Saturday.
       A   B   C   D

8. <u>That</u> <u>running</u> shoes are great, but <u>that</u> shirt <u>looks</u> terrible.
    A   B   C   D

9. Many years <u>ago</u>, women wore <u>hats</u> and <u>glove</u> all day and all <u>evening</u>.
               A   B   C   D

10. <u>Children</u> <u>usually</u> love TV shows with music, <u>dancing</u>, and a <u>lots</u> of color.
      A   B   C   D

11. I wanted to buy <u>something</u> for <u>hers</u> birthday, but <u>the</u> store wasn't <u>open</u>.
                  A   B   C   D

12. <u>How</u> long <u>are</u> you <u>going</u> to <u>studied</u>?
   A   B   C   D

13. There wasn't <u>no</u> food <u>at</u> the party, but <u>they</u> stayed.
    A   B   C   D

14. <u>This</u> <u>students</u> like to <u>go</u> <u>biking</u> on the weekends.
    A   B   C   D

15. <u>Any</u> <u>students</u> feel <u>nervous</u> in front of <u>the</u> class.
    A   B   C   D

SECTION 5
Reading

> 1. Read the passage.
> 2. Read the question.
> 3. Circle the letter of the best answer.

Questions 1–5

Yo-Yo Ma is a famous cellist who gives concerts all over the world. He has made over one hundred recordings—everything from Chinese music to tangos.

Ma's parents left China in the 1930s. His father, Hiao-Tsun Ma, was a music historian. Ma was born in Paris in 1955. He began studying the cello when he was four. In 1962, the family moved to New York City, and Ma grew up there.

Ma has a famous cello that was made in the eighteenth century. One time, Ma accidentally left the cello in a taxi in New York. He was worried about the loss of his instrument. Fortunately, the taxi driver noticed the cello, called Ma, and returned it to him.

Ma and his wife, Jill, have two children, Nicholas and Emily. Ma's life is exciting. Playing the cello is hard work, but he always has time for his family.

1. What is the *topic* of this passage?

(A) A history of cello music
(B) Yo-Yo Ma's life in music
(C) Music in New York City
(D) The new Chinese music

2. According to the passage, what is *true* about Ma?

   (A) Ma's cello was broken in a taxi.
   (B) Ma's mother was a homemaker.
   (C) Ma plays in many countries.
   (D) Ma's children have musical talent.

3. What is *stated* in the passage about Ma's family?

   (A) His wife is from the United States.
   (B) His father was a doctor.
   (C) His family moved in 1962.
   (D) His sister plays the piano.

4. What is *probably true* about Ma's cello?

   (A) It cost a lot of money.
   (B) Ma lost the cello in Paris.
   (C) Ma bought it when he was four.
   (D) It is a new cello.

5. What is a good *title* for this passage?

   (A) A World-Famous Cellist
   (B) The Story of a Famous Cello
   (C) Great Music Historians in China
   (D) Yo-Yo Ma's Unhappy Life

Questions 6–10

   Around the world, people spend their free time in many different ways. In Italy, there's a wonderful custom called the *passegiatta*.

   Imagine a small Italian town on a hot, sunny, summer day. During the afternoon, people are indoors. It's too hot to be outside. Everything is quiet. Slowly, afternoon turns into evening. As the day cools, people come out for a walk. It's time for the *passegiatta*.

   During the *passegiatta*, people of all ages stroll along with friends or family members. As they walk, they talk and laugh. They stop to talk to friends and neighbors along the way. Many people stop at a small restaurant or café for a cup of coffee or for some ice cream called *gelato*. They stay there a while to chat with friends.

   The evening walk is a time to relax and visit with friends, neighbors, and relatives. It's a chance to meet and talk about what is happening in town and around the world.

6. What is the topic of this passage?

   (A) dating services in Italy
   (B) an Italian custom
   (C) the weather in Italy
   (D) an advertisement for tourists

7. According to the passage, what is *probably true* about the *passegiatta*?

    (A) It is only for young people.
    (B) It always takes place before breakfast.
    (C) It is a chance for young people to meet.
    (D) It takes place once a year.

8. According to the passage, what do people *do* during the *passegiatta*?

    (A) They stay at home and they watch television.
    (B) They go outside and walk around together.
    (C) They spend a lot of time playing sports.
    (D) They talk to their relatives on the telephone.

9. According to the passage, which statement is *true*?

    (A) Everyone in Italy drinks coffee and eats gelato.
    (B) Italians take walks only in the winter.
    (C) Gelato is a kind of coffee.
    (D) This custom takes place in the evening.

10. What is the *main idea* of this passage?

    (A) The *passegiatta* is a way to relax and visit with friends.
    (B) Italy is a wonderful place to go on vacation.
    (C) Italian men don't like to visit with friends.
    (D) People have the same customs all around the world.